THE BEST WAYS TO WIN FRIENDS AND INFLUENCE PEOPLE

By Michelle W. Bartolome

Table Of Contents

Chapter 1

The Great Human Relations Secret

There is only one way in heaven to get anybody to do anything. Have you ever given it any thought? A single method, yes. Making the other person want to do it is how you do this.

Recall that there is no other option.

Of course, putting a gun in a man's rib cage will make him want to hang up his watch. When you threaten to terminate a worker, they will cooperate with you until you turn around. A whip or a threat will get a kid to do what you want them to. These imprecise techniques, however, have very unfavorable effects.

Giving you what you want is the only way I can persuade you to do anything. What would you like?

Every action you and I take is motivated by two desires: the desire to have sex and the desire to be successful, according to the renowned Dr. Sigmund Freud of Vienna, one of the most illustrious psychiatrists of the twentieth century.

The most learned philosopher in America, Professor John Dewey, puts it another way. According to Dr. Dewey, "the need to be significant" is the basic instinct that drives human nature. "The yearning to be important"—remember that? It is important. It will come up quite a bit in this book.

What would you like? You don't want many things, but the ones that you do want, you insist on getting with an unyielding lust. Almost all average adults desire:

- Life preservation and good health
- Food.
- Sleep.
- The items that can be purchased with money
- Existence in the afterlife.
- Pleasure on a sexual level.
- The health and safety of our kids.
- A sense of significance

Except for one, almost all of these desires are satisfied. However, there is one want that is seldom satiated and is nearly as intense and demanding as the need for food or sleep. Freud referred to it as "the drive to be great." Dewey refers to it as "the wish to be significant."

Everyone enjoys praise, as Lincoln once said at the opening of a letter. "The underlying essence of human nature is the yearning to be recognized," observed William James. He didn't mention the "want," "desire," or "longing" to be respected, mind you. He said that the "craving" should be valued.

The rare person who really feeds this heart need will have others in the palm of his hand, and "even the undertaker will be sad when he dies." This is a persistent and unyielding human yearning.

One of the key distinctions between humans and other animals is the need for a sense of significance. For instance: My father raised magnificent Duroc-Jersey pigs and purebred white-faced cattle when I was a young farm child in Missouri. In the past, we used to display our hogs and white-faced cattle at rural fairs and livestock competitions around the Middle West. By a large margin, we took first place.

When company or visitors arrived at the house, my father would pull out the long piece of muslin that he had attached his blue ribbons to. While he displayed the blue ribbons, he would hold one end while I held the other.

The ribbons the pigs earned didn't matter to them. It was, however, Father.These awards made him feel important.

Civilization would not have been feasible if our forefathers had not had this burning need for a sense of significance. Without it, humans ought to have been quite similar to animals.

This need for a sense of significance motivated an illiterate, underprivileged supermarket cashier to read some legal books he discovered in the bottom of a bucket of domestic loot he had purchased for fifty cents. Most likely, you've heard of this grocery store employee. Lincoln was his name.

Dickens' enduring books were driven by his need for a sense of significance. Sir Christopher Wren was motivated by this urge to create his stone symphonies. Rockefeller accumulated millions that he never spent due to this ambition! The wealthiest guy in your community also built a mansion that was far too big for him out of the same ambition.

You want to speak about your smart kids, drive the newest automobile, and wear the newest fashions because of this ambition.

Many boys and girls are drawn to become gangsters and shooters by this urge. According to E. P. Mulrooney, a former police commissioner of New York, "the ordinary young criminal of today is full of ego, and his first request after arrest is for those colorful tabloids that make him out to be a hero." As long as he can take pride in the fact that images of Babe Ruth, La-Gaurdia, Einstein, Lindbergh, Toscanini, or Roosevelt are shown beside his visage, the unappealing possibility of doing a "hot squat" in the electric chair appears far away. "I'll tell you what you are if you tell me where you got the idea that you're important." Your character is determined by it. The most important quality about you is that John D. Rockefeller, for instance, receives his sense of significance from funding the construction of a cutting-edge hospital in Peking, China, to care for millions of destitute people he has never seen and will never meet.

Dillinger, on the other hand, acquired his sense of significance from his criminal activities as a bandit, robber, and murderer. He sprinted inside a farmhouse up in Minnesota while the G-men were after him and shouted, "I'm Dillinger!" He took great pride in becoming the public's number one enemy. "I won't injure you, but I'm Dillinger," he said.

Yes, how Dillinger and Rockefeller acquired their sense of significance is the one key distinction between them.

Funny instances of prominent individuals battling for a sense of significance may be seen throughout history. Columbus argued that he should be named "Admiral of the Ocean and Viceroy of India," and even George Washington desired to be called "His Mightiness, the President of the United States." When letters were not addressed to "Her Imperial Majesty," Catherine the Great would not read them, and Mrs. Lincoln turned on Mrs. Grant in the White House like a tigress and said, "How dare you be seated in my presence before I ask you?"

With the understanding that icy mountain ranges would be named after them, our millionaires contributed to Admiral Byrd's Antarctic expedition's funding, and Victor Hugo wanted nothing less than the city of Paris to be renamed in his honor. Even Shakespeare, the most powerful of the powerful, made an effort to enhance his reputation by obtaining a coat of arms for his family.

Sometimes people pretend to be disabled in order to attract sympathy and attention and feel important. For instance, consider Mrs. McKinley. By making her husband, the President of the United States, neglect crucial matters of state while he sat on the bed next to her for hours at a time, his arm around her, lulling her to sleep, she gained a sense of importance. She made sure he was by her side while she had her teeth fixed, feeding her gnawing need for attention. She once caused a commotion when he had to leave her with the dentist while he had an appointment with John Hay.

Mary Roberts Rinehart once related to me the story of a smart, active young lady who decided to become an invalid in order to feel important. According to Mrs. Rinehart, the lady had to confront something, maybe her age or the knowledge that she would never get married feel important. According to Mrs. Rinehart, the lady had to confront something, maybe her age or the knowledge that she would never get married. There wasn't much left for her to look forward to as the lonely years stretched out before her. She climbed into bed, and for 10 years, her elderly mother carried trays while nursing her on her way to and from the third floor. The elderly mother eventually passed away after being worn out from her duties. The invalid sat around for a few weeks before getting up, dressing herself, and starting to live again.

The sense of significance that has been denied to them in the harsh world of reality, according to some experts, may cause individuals to truly go mad. In the US, people with mental illnesses outnumber those with all other illnesses combined. The likelihood that you will spend seven years of your life in an insane institution if you are over fifteen and live in New York State is one in twenty.

What triggers mental illness?

Nobody can respond to such a broad question, but we do know that certain illnesses, like syphilis, damage and kill brain cells, leading to insanity. In reality, physical factors including brain lesions, alcohol, poisons, and traumas account for nearly half of all mental illnesses. However, the other half of those who go mad, and this is the horrifying part of the talee the other half of those who go insane seem to have normal, healthy brain cells. They seem to have brain tissues that are just as healthy as yours and mine when examined after death using the most powerful microscopes.

Why do these folks lose their minds?

I recently asked the chief physician of one of our most significant hospitals that question. This distinguished physician, who has won several prizes for his expertise in insanity, was honest when he informed me that he had no idea why individuals were mad. Nobody can be certain. He did, however, mention that many individuals who lose their minds have a sense of significance in madness that they are unable to experience in the world of truth.

Then he began to tell me this tale: "I now have a patient whose marriage turned out to be a catastrophe. She desired love, sex, children, and social status, but reality dashed all of her expectations. Her spouse didn't care about her. She was forced to serve him meals in his upstairs room since he wouldn't even sit down to dine with her. She was socially inept and had no children. As a result of her mental illness, she divorced her husband and reverted to using her maiden name. She insists on being referred to as Lady Smith since she now thinks she has married into the English nobility.

And as for kids, she imagines that she has had a new one every night at this point. She always answers the phone by saying, "Doctor, I had a baby last night."

All of life's dream ships were once shattered on the jagged rocks of reality, but now all of her barkentines speed into port with sails billowing and breezes humming through the masts.

Tragic? Oh, I have no idea. Her doctor told me, "If I could reach out and give her back her sanity, I wouldn't." She is a lot happier as she is right now.

People who are mad are often happier than we are. Many people like being crazy. Exactly why not? Their issues have been resolved. They will either offer you a check for $1 million or an introduction letter to the Aga Khan. The sense of significance they so desperately sought has been obtained in the fantasy world they have created. Imagine the marvels you and I can work if we show people that there are some individuals who are so desperate for a sense of significance that they would do everything to attain it.

I am aware of just two individuals who have ever received a salary of $1 million: Walter Chrysler and Charles Schwab.

Why did Andrew Carnegie pay Schwab $1 million a year, or almost $3,000 per day? Why?

due to Schwab's genius? No. because he was more knowledgeable than others about how steel is made? Nonsense. Charles Schwab admitted to me that he had numerous employees who were more knowledgeable than he was regarding the production of steel.

According to Schwab, the main reason he received this compensation was for his interpersonal skills. I questioned him on his method. Here is his secret, as described in his own words. These are the words that should be immortalized in eternal bronze and hung in every home, school, business, and office across the nation. Children should memorize these words rather than wasting their time learning Latin verb conjugations or Brazil's annual rainfall amounts. These are the words that, if we choose to live them, will essentially change our lives.

The finest quality in a guy may be developed through recognition and encouragement, according to Schwab, who said that his capacity to inspire men is his greatest strength.

Nothing else destroys a man's goals as quickly as criticism from his superiors. I never make someone feel bad. I think it's important to motivate men to work. I thus hesitate to criticize but am eager to appreciate. If there is something that I admire, I will give it my wholehearted approval and profuse praise.

Schwab operates in this manner. What does the typical male do, though? just the opposite: He raises the Old Harry when he doesn't like something and says nothing when he does.

"I have yet to find the man, however great or exalted his station, who did not do better work and put forth greater effort under a spirit of approval than he would ever do under a spirit of criticism," Schwab said. "Throughout my long life, I have met many great men from all over the world."

He said that one of the most notable causes of Andrew Carnegie's extraordinary success was what he stated. Both in public and in private, Carnegie gave his colleagues accolades.

Even on his gravestone, Carnegie wanted to mention how great his helpers were. "Here sleeps one who knew how to gather around him guys who were cleverer than himself," his tombstone for himself said.

One of the keys to Rockefeller's success in managing men was sincere admiration. For instance, John D. could have reprimanded Edward T. Bedford, one of his partners, when Bedford pulled a fast one and cost the company $1 million via a poor purchase in South America, but he understood Bedford had done his best and the matter was resolved. Rockefeller therefore found a reason to commend Bedford, praising him for being able to preserve 60% of the money he had invested. "That's wonderful," Rockefeller said. "We don't usually perform so well upstairs," The most magnificent businessman to ever amaze Broadway, Ziegfeld made his name by deftly "glorifying the

American girl." He often took some unattractive little creature that no one ever paid much attention to and turned her into a gorgeous image of mystery and seduction on stage. He made women feel attractive by the sheer force of his gallantry and attention because he understood the value of praise and confidence. He was realistic; he increased the chorus ladies' weekly pay from thirty dollars to as much as one hundred and seventy-five dollars. He was also chivalrous; on the Follies' opening night, he sent telegrams to the cast members and showered American Beauty flowers on each chorus member.

I once gave in to the fasting craze and skipped meals for six days and nights. It wasn't challenging. At the conclusion of the sixth day, I felt less hungry than I had at the end of the first. However, I know and you know people who would consider it a crime if they allowed their families or employees to go without food for six days; however, they will allow them to go for six days, six weeks, and occasionally sixty years without showing them the heartfelt appreciation that they yearn for almost as much as food.

There is nothing I need more than food for my self-esteem, said Alfred Lunt, who portrayed the lead in Reunion in Vienna.

We feed our friends' and coworkers' bodies, but how seldom do we feed their self-esteem? We feed them roast steak and potatoes to keep them going, but we forget to compliment them with words that will ring in their ears like the dawn symphony for years.

As they read these sentences, some people are exclaiming, "Old crap! supple soap! Flattery from a Bear!I have used those things. It doesn't work, at least not with smart people.

Of course, flattery seldom resonates with intelligent individuals. It is unauthentic, self-serving, and superficial. It should fail, as it often does. It's true that some individuals are so thirsty for approval and so hungry for food that they'll eat anything, much as a starving person would eat grass and fish worms.

How come the often-wed Mdivani brothers were such blazing successes in the marriage market, for instance? Why were these so-called "princes" able to wed two gorgeous and well-

known movie actresses, a legendary prima donna, and Barbara Hutton with her millions from the five-and-ten-cent store? Why? Why did they succeed?
According to Adela Rogers St. Johns in an article published in the journal Liberty, the Mdivani charm for ladies has long been one of mankind's greatest secrets.
It was once told to me by the worldly, shrewd, and talented artist Pola Negri. She observed, "They are the only guys I have ever met who really understand the art of flatteryhey are the only guys I have ever met who really understand the art of flattery." And in today's satirical and realistic world, the art of flattery is all but abandoned. "That, I can guarantee you, is the Mdivani charm for women's magic formula. I know."
Even Queen Victoria was a sucker for compliments. Disraeli, the prime minister, acknowledged that he overreached while interacting with the Queen. He specifically said that he "spread it on with a trowel." But Disraeli was among the most refined, skillful, and shrewd leaders of the vast British Empire. In his field, he was brilliant. For you and me, what worked for him may not necessarily work for

you. Over time, flattery will actually work against you. Flattery is fake, and if you attempt to pass it off as real, it will ultimately get you in hot water.

What separates flattery from appreciation? That is easy. The one is genuine, while the other is not. One originates from the bottom of the heart, the other from the top. One person is selfless, whereas the other is. One is generally praised, whereas everyone despises the other.

I just came upon a bust of General Obregon at Mexico City's Chapultepec Palace. General Obregon's sage advice is engraved under the bust: "Don't be terrified of adversaries who assault you." Be cautious about flattering friends.

Not at all! I'm not advocating flattery here! Not at all. I'm referring to a new way of living. I'll say it again. I'm referring to a new way of living.

Six maxims were posted on the walls of King George V's study at Buckingham Palace. "Teach me not to give or accept cheap praise," read one of these adages. All flattery consists of cheap praise. Perhaps it's worth reiterating the best definition of flattery I ever read: "Flattery is telling the other guy exactly what he thinks about himself."

Ralph Waldo Emerson once observed, "Use whatever language you choose; you can never communicate anything but what you are."

Everyone would figure it out if we just used flattery, and we should all be social relations specialists by now.

We typically spend around 95% of our time thinking about ourselves when we are not thinking about some specific issue. Now, if we temporarily put ourselves out of our minds and focus on the positive qualities of the other man, we won't need to use flattery that is so shoddy and false that it is detected almost before it leaves our mouths.

Every man I meet is, in some way, my superior, and I learn from him, according to Emerson.

If that were true of Emerson, wouldn't it be a million times more likely to be true of you and me? Let's stop focusing on our goals and accomplishments. Let's try to identify the positive aspects of the other man. So disregard flattery. express sincere gratitude that is genuine. People will treasure and repeat your words for a lifetime, even years after you have forgotten them, if you are "hearty in your approval and lavish in your praise."

Chapter 2

A Strong First Impression

When you first meet someone, it only takes three seconds for them to form an opinion of you. The other person forms an opinion about you in this little period of time based on your look, body language, temperament, mannerisms, and how you are dressed.
Every time you interact with someone new, they assess you and form an opinion of you. These initial impressions often set the tone for the relationship that follows and may be very difficult to change or undo.
Use the five suggestions in this video and narrative to make a terrific first impression.
Consequently, it's crucial that you understand how to make a terrific first impression. To assist you in doing this, this article offers some helpful advice.
Making a good first impression

1. Be punctual

Your "nice explanation" for being late won't intrigue someone you are meeting for the first time. Plan to arrive a few minutes early and leave yourself some leeway in case of traffic delays or a wrong turn. Being on time is the first step in making a strong first impression and is far preferable to arriving late.
Check your gear and connection in advance if your first encounter is virtual, and consider your surroundings and background.

2. Display yourself respectfully.

Of course, looks are important. When you meet someone for the first time, they don't know you, so the first thing they notice about you is often how you look.
But don't be alarmed! This does not imply that you must be flawless to make a powerful and favorable first impression. (Except, of course, if you are interviewing with your neighborhood modeling agency.)

No. Making a good impression is all about how you portray yourself.
Since a picture is worth a thousand words, the "image" you initially give to a new acquaintance must reflect who you are.
First, consider your clothing choices. What kind of attire is acceptable for the meeting or situation? What kind of clothing should you wear in a professional setting? suit, blazer, or casual attire? What kind of clothing is the person you're meeting likely to be wearing? A pinstripe business suit may not be the best choice if your contact works in the performing or visual arts.
When in a foreign environment or nation, you should pay special attention to the appropriate attire for business and social encounters since it differs between cultures. Make sure you are familiar with the customs and traditions of the country and culture you are visiting.

3. Be who you are.

Yes, you do need to "blend in" a little bit if you want to make a good impression. However, it does not include becoming someone you are not or losing who you are. Being true to who you are is the best way to make an impact. You'll feel more certain, be able to establish trust, and gain the respect and integrity of the individuals you encounter if you do this.

4. Display a glorious smile!

"Smile, and the world smiles too," as the adage goes. So nothing makes a good first impression like a grin. A kind grin that exudes confidence will put the other individual at ease. So when it comes to making a good first impression, smiling wins. But be careful not to overdo it; those who do so risk coming off as smarmy and fake.

5. Be frank and assured.

It's frequently true that body language conveys more information than words when it comes to generating a strong first impression.
Use your body language to convey the right amount of certainty and confidence. Make eye contact, stand

tall, smile (of course), and extend a solid handshake in greeting. All of this will support your confidence-projecting efforts and make you and the other person feel more comfortable.

When meeting someone for the first time, almost everyone has some degree of nerves. However, this could result in undesirable side effects, including sweaty hands, the "jitters," or nail biting. You may attempt to control your anxious tendencies by becoming aware of them. For assistance with this, go to our page on relaxing methods.

6. Make Small Talk

With verbal give and take, conversations are built. Asking the individual you are meeting some questions in advance could be helpful. Alternatively, spend a few minutes getting to know them. Do they, for instance, play golf? Do they collaborate with a nearby nonprofit organization? Do you have any similarities with them? If so, doing so may be a terrific way to start and maintain a discussion. Be optimistic.

All of your actions exhibit a positive mindset. So, even while feeling frightened or facing criticism, present an optimistic attitude. Make an effort to absorb meeting information and provide useful input. Finally, keep your attitude positive and smile to convey that you are accessible.

8. Show respect and pay attention.

It goes without saying that having good manners and acting in an attentive, polite, and courteous manner aid in creating a positive first impression. In fact, if you do anything less, it might sabotage your one opportunity to make a good first impression. Do your best to behave, then!

To offer the individual your whole attention, put away contemporary distractions, such as turning off your cell phone. Likewise, avoid being distracted by others. After all, if you are more interested in chatting with someone else, what sort of first impression would you make? Your whole focus should be on your new friend. Anything less will probably cause them to feel ignored or even annoyed.

Improve your communication abilities.

Making connections, establishing relationships, and working effectively all require the ability to initiate and sustain conversations. For the rest of us, conversational skills must be developed and honed since some individuals appear to be conversationalists by nature. In this post, we provide six tested strategies for improving communication skills.

What characteristics exactly define a good conversationalist?

Even though some individuals appear to be inherently charming, if you know what you want to get out of the discussion, you can learn how to do it. Here are five traits of an effective conversationalist:

listening intently

You can tell when the person you're speaking to is giving you their complete attention. They're focused on you and want to interact with you rather than merely hear what you have to say.

Questioning

It naturally piques interest to pay close attention to someone who is speaking, which prompts clarifying queries. People who are listening to you often have questions because they are curious to learn more.

They provide inquiries that further broaden the scope of the discussion and give you the chance to elaborate on your points and voice your viewpoints. They keep eye contact with you while you respond to their queries, demonstrating their interest in your tale even more.

Self-disclosure

By opening up and responding in turn, the other person is encouraged to do the same. A fantastic way to start a discussion and build ties with people is to share a personal tidbit.

This is something that a skilled conversationalist is aware of, and they also know how much to discuss and when to stop. They are adept at starting with an intriguing fact, such as a favorite book, television program, or sports team. While not extremely intimate, these topics are excellent conversation starters when trying to get to know someone.

Accepting silence

A skilled conversationalist is aware that not all pauses are uncomfortable. A slowdown in the conversation may not necessarily imply that it has ended; instead, it may be a sign that it is time to refocus and get ready for the next round of debate. When the speaker is speaking, it is also much appreciated if the listener remains silent. An excellent conversationalist listens just as much as they speak, if not more.

Being considerate

If there is one quality that unites all successful conversationalists, it is civility. The only way to maintain a meaningful discussion is to act politely and respect the other person. Avoiding interruptions, listening intently, refraining from talking too much about oneself, and not glancing at one's phone are all characteristics of polite discourse.

Why is having a smooth conversation essential?

Humans naturally gravitate toward discussion because it allows us to get to know one another, exchange ideas, and satisfy our desire for social connection. Being a great conversationalist may provide a much richer experience for you and the people you chat with, which can foster rewarding relationships, mutual understanding, and creativity. Conversation is essential to everyday living.

Brain stimulation, creative stimulation, and global connection are all benefits of conversation. By developing your conversational skills, you may provide others with the same rewarding experience by engaging their minds, fostering their creativity, and building relationships with them. This stimulation may promote more effective problem-solving, more happiness, and a better comprehension of subjects you previously knew nothing about.

By giving your coworkers and those close to you a forum to exchange thoughts, express grievances, provide or receive advice, and generally experience improved mental health, being a good conversationalist supports them. The path to successful idea development and teamwork, both

individually and collectively, is conversation.
Use the advice below to start enhancing your speaking abilities:

1. Begin with bantering.

Simple, cursory communication is the best way to learn how to have conversations. A fantastic method to get experience interacting on deeper levels is via small talk. For instance, a casual remark made to a stranger about the weather might lead to a deeper conversation and lifetime connections.

2. Describe yourself

Introduce yourself when that casual remark about the weather turns into a full-blown discussion. You may think about doing the typical introduction where you tell them a little bit about yourself to start a discussion, or you could just extend your hand and say your name. In any case, you've moved on to what might be a very interesting discussion.

3. Discover a similar ground

Even if your only thing in common is that you're both in the same area at the same time, it's often reasonable to presume that you have something else in common when you find yourself in the same location as someone else. If you want to start a discussion, find out how they got here. For instance, it might be beneficial to find out what other organizations you could support if you meet someone at the same charity event you are attending.

4. Pose open-ended inquiries.

Ask open-ended questions to elicit additional information from the individual if they seem interested in speaking with you but are only responding with affirmative or negative statements. When following up with inquiries like "What is that like?" or "How did you accomplish that?" keep the five Ws in mind to encourage them to reflect more deeply on the experience they just shared with you. By demonstrating your sincere interest in them, you're more likely to encourage them to actively participate in the discussion.

5. Pay attention to your dialogue partner.

Picking up your phone and starting to scroll or text is one of the easiest ways to show that you are not interested in what is being said. Additionally, by dividing your attention, you lose concentration on the discussion, which makes the experience much less fulfilling for both you and the other person. Avoid multitasking and give your discussion partner your whole attention in order to gain and deliver the best experience possible. Ask meaningful questions, really listen, and avoid interjecting.

6. express your gratitude.

When you finish talking, let the other person know how much you enjoyed hearing from them. To further demonstrate your attention, bring up anything someone said, such as "I appreciate you providing the name of your technician." "I'll ask him to check my brakes." This small act can go a long way toward making someone feel valued and opening the door for future conversations. Give each other your cards or your phone numbers, and then get in touch with them a few days later.

Chapter 3

How to increase your interest level as a person

To keep people's attention, you don't need to be a millionaire, CEO, or astronaut; you may just be you.

It comes down to learning how to draw attention to the qualities that set you apart from the person standing next to you.

How can I become a more fascinating person? is a topic that dozens of individuals have provided answers to based on their own experiences. We selected the most useful tips after sorting through their comments.

Continue reading to learn how to persuade others—and, more crucially, yourself—that you are an interesting person.

1. Acquire new abilities

Make sure others find you intriguing by being helpful on every occasion. Anthony N. Lee, a Quora user, advises acquiring as many practical skills as you can, from web design to sewing.
In this manner, you'll always be a friend's first choice should they need someone to design a website for their new company or a blanket for their infant niece.

2. Show interest

By excluding other people's ideas and perspectives, you may make sure you're not interesting. Instead, you should actively look for fresh perspectives and encounters that will alter the way you feel and think.
Being a "lifelong learner" is something that Sudhir Desai promotes. He advises keeping an open mind and being interested.Recognize that there are many different ways to view the

world. Learn new information to widen and develop your worldview.

3. Develop your storytelling skills.

Even if you have a ton of knowledge and expertise, if you can't share it with others, you're doomed.

You should develop your storytelling skills because, in Marcus Geduld's words, "you don't simply pour whatever is on your mind into the discussion; you actively structure it to make it engaging." Begin to see your life as a gift you may bestow on others. Wrap it in the best paper you can find.

In order to tease your listeners with hints about the resolution of the narrative, Geduld advises learning how to read your audience to determine how long they will be able to pay attention.

It's interesting to note that a recent study discovered that women find guys who can tell a good tale to be more appealing. According to the study's authors, this may be because great storytellers may appear to be in a better position to persuade others or obtain power.

4. Prepare three excellent tales to tell.

Being able to tell a tale on the spot is useful, but if you're hesitant, prepare yourself with a few personal experiences you may use to spice up a routine conversation.
"Comedians don't simply speak about anything while they're onstage," Devesh writes. They have practiced their performance. A job interview is not a place where you can just walk in and say whatever comes to mind.Always have three solid tales on hand that will consistently amuse, educate, or interest.

5. Pay attention and be sympathetic.

By showing interest in others, you can create more friends in two months than you can in two years of attempting to pique their interest.
Pay close attention to what people are saying and make an effort to

empathize with their intentions. Very few of us are really skilled at this. If we listen to everyone with an adequate imagination, their experience of life becomes almost unlimited. By figuring it out, we develop. Also helpful is wondering whether you're mistaken.

6. Pose thoughtful questions.

You don't have to talk much about yourself at a party for others to find you fascinating. Instead, have in-depth discussions with them about their way of life.

As necessary, inquire carefully (but not intrusively) about them, their hobbies, and their top priorities, advises Stephanie Vardavas. Pay close attention to the responses. Follow up with additional in-depth dialogue and appropriate inquiries (again, not prying). By the end of the night, they will consider you to be among the most fascinating individuals they have ever encountered.

Don't be ashamed to ask questions that seem obvious. Pretending to know something when you don't usually serves no purpose. The objective of a reporter is to obtain facts, not to astound their subjects. Business shouldn't be any different, but it isn't. You can wind up impressing your new pals by asking those basic queries.

7. Express your opinions.

Boring people are those who have no opinions or don't disagree with anything. "You feel as if you can never truly talk to them," she writes. "You should strive to express your true opinions on some subjects, even if others won't agree with you."

8. Pursue your passions.

Consider studying things that you truly find fascinating rather than a ton of boring subjects just to appear educated. When discussing things with others, you'll seem lively and interesting if you do it that way.
Being an ardent learner and gatherer of knowledge that interests and thrills you, I don't believe it's so much a question of trying to be intriguing as it is of naturally doing what you like.

Reading often helps you develop an engaging and sympathetic view of the world.

9. Read widely

It's excellent if you have the time and resources to tour the globe. But even if you don't, reading whatever you can get your hands on will still help you learn about other cultures and historical eras.
Expose yourself to as many fresh tales and concepts as you can via books, blogs, and journals.
According to Keith Oatley's evaluation of the last ten years' worth of studies on the psychological consequences of reading fiction, "people who read more fiction were better at evoking empathy and understanding others."

10. Show your sense of humor.

Awdesh Singh advises incorporating humor into your relationships with other people. Learn to find the humor in everything, he advises, and make it

a point to smile even when things go wrong.
If you're looking to impress a date, bonus: According to research, women find amusing guys more appealing, probably because they come across as smarter.

11. Spend time with intriguing others.

Singh continues by saying that your social circle has an impact on your personality. You're likely to quickly start acting like them if you hang around with dull, grumpy, or serious folks, the speaker warns. The same holds true if you are among intriguing folks.
Consider affiliating with a Meetup group or similar association of people driven to follow their hobbies and passions.

12. Focus on a particular interest of yours.

You could be tempted to dabble in a variety of subjects and learn a little bit about everything. Instead, think about becoming really knowledgeable about one subject and showcasing your mastery of it.

"When someone genuinely pursues one subject with tremendous passion and depth over a long period of time," says April Fonti, she finds them to be engaging. They could be brilliant scientists or simply reserved loners. It is irrelevant. Your communication abilities may be enhanced by learning improvisational techniques.

13. Attend a lesson in improv.

Your ability to communicate in everyday situations may be enhanced by engaging in improvisational training. It improves your listening skills since you pay more attention to what the other person is saying than to what you're going to say next.

Even if you're timid and don't plan to perform in front of an audience, comic improv will help you loosen up, think more quickly, rediscover your sense of playfulness (which most adults have lost), and feel more at ease embarrassing yourself in front of others (a life skill that comes in handy frequently). It may help you open up and become more involved in social interactions.

14. Display originality

Being different from everyone else is essential to being fascinating.After college, a friend of mine did something that had never been done before (at least that I was aware of).He walked around the island's shoreline and beach. It simply required a few days and some camping equipment. He still tells the story twenty years later.
However, not everyone is now equipped or motivated to go on a record-breaking camping expedition. Therefore, reflect on the peculiar experiences you've previously experienced. You may have lived abroad, sold art as a side business, or had ten siblings when you were a child. Keep looking; something is there for sure.

15. Accept your oddity.

"We all have our peculiarities," says Del Singh. It is intrinsic to who we are.

People who are interesting let their inner quirkiness out.
We're no longer in junior high school, so dressing, speaking, and behaving like everyone else may become a little monotonous. Therefore, fly the freak flag with confidence.

16. Be approachable

Danielle Lan tells a personal tale, and the lesson is that you have to tell others how intriguing you are for them to find out. "My spouse has been characterized as dull." With all his peculiarities and interests, he is a very intriguing individual. He never shares with his employees or friends, which is an issue. His standard response to questions about his weekend is, "Fine."He most likely participated in a major raid in his preferred MMO [massively multiplayer online game] before seeing a brand-new film and reading a fascinating book. But he's not going to tell just anyone.
You must share if you want to be seen as interesting. You must therefore have stuff to share, so to speak. Rare indeed is the individual who does nothing at

all and has no views whatsoever. My suggestion is to be honest.

In fact, research reveals that when two individuals share a personal moment together rather than when just one does, people get along better.

17. Join a different group of people.

Perhaps spending time with individuals who don't value you is the underlying cause of your lack of interest. If so, you need to look for a new community that appreciates everything that you have to give.

How to instantly win people over

It might be difficult to explain why you like someone.
Perhaps it's their silly grin; perhaps it's their incisive wit; perhaps it's just that they're fun to be around. You just enjoy them.
Scientists have spent years attempting to identify the precise variables that compel one individual to choose another, but they are often unsatisfied with replies like that.

We've included some of their most fascinating discoveries here. Continue reading for information that can help you build stronger connections more quickly and see your present friendships in a fresh light.

1. Make a copy of your companion

This tactic, known as "mirroring," involves carefully imitating another person's actions. Try to mimic the motions, facial expressions, and body language of the person you are speaking to.

Researchers from New York University first identified the "chameleon effect" in 1999, which is when individuals unintentionally imitate one another's behavior. That imitation makes anything appealing.

72 male and female participants were given an assignment to complete with a partner. While researchers recorded the encounters, the partners (who worked for the researchers) either imitated the other participant's behavior or didn't. The participants were asked to rate how much they

loved their partners after the encounter.

Indeed, when their spouse imitated their behavior, participants were more likely to claim that they loved their companion.

2. Spend more time with the folks you want to become friends with.

The mere-exposure effect states that individuals have a tendency to like those who are acquainted with them.

Psychologists at the University of Pittsburgh had four women pretend to be students in a college psychology class as one illustration of this occurrence. Various women attended class on different occasions. Male students displayed a larger affinity for the woman they had seen more often in class when experimenters showed them images of the four women, even though they hadn't interacted with any of them.

3. Give others praise.

The adjectives you choose to describe other individuals will be linked to your personality by others. Spontaneous trait transmission is the name for this occurrence.
This impact was discovered by one piece of research that was published in the Journal of Personality and Social Psychology, even though individuals were aware that particular attributes didn't apply to the people who had spoken about them.
The Happiness Project author Gretchen Rubin asserts that "anything you say about other people effects how others regard you."
People will relate to you as sincere and nice if you characterize someone else in such terms. The opposite is also true: If you frequently criticize individuals behind their backs, your friends will begin to think the same thing about you.

4. attempt to exhibit optimistic feelings.

The term "emotional contagion" refers to the phenomenon wherein individuals are significantly impacted

by the emotions of others. People may instinctively sense the emotions of individuals around them, according to a study from Ohio University and the University of Hawaii.
The authors of the study speculate that this may be because we often replicate the actions and expressions of others, which causes us to experience similar emotions. Try your best to convey cheerful feelings to others if you want them to feel joyful around you.

5. exude warmth and expertise.

The stereotype content model, which postulates that individuals evaluate others based on their friendliness and competence, was developed by psychologists at Princeton University and their colleagues.
According to the model, people will feel like they can trust you if you can present yourself as warm, kind, and noncompetitive. They are more likely to respect you if you seem knowledgeable, for instance, or if you have a high level of economic or educational prestige.
According to Harvard psychologist Amy Cuddy, it's crucial to show

warmth before skill, particularly in professional contexts.
According to Cuddy, it is more essential to our survival from an evolutionary standpoint to determine if a person earns our confidence.

6. Periodically disclose your shortcomings.

The pratfall effect states that when you make a mistake, people will like you more—but only if they think you are a competent person. You become more relatable and vulnerable to others around you when you admit your flaws.
This effect was initially identified by University of Texas at Austin researcher Elliot Aronson while researching how inadvertent errors might change how attractive someone is considered. He requested that University of Minnesota male students listen to recordings of individuals taking a test.
The students gave those who performed well on the quiz but spilled coffee at the conclusion of the interview a higher likability rating than those who performed poorly on the

quiz or did not do well on the quiz and spilled coffee.

7. Highlight common values.

A famous study by Theodore Newcomb found that individuals are more drawn to others who are like them. The similarity-attraction effect is what's behind this. In his study, Newcomb assessed the opinions of his participants toward touchy topics like politics and sex before placing them in a residence owned by the University of Michigan to live together.

When their roommates exhibited comparable opinions about the topics studied at the conclusion of their stay, the participants grew to enjoy them more.

It's worth noting that a more recent study conducted by researchers at the University of Virginia and Washington University in St. Louis discovered that recruits in the Air Force liked each other more when they shared negative personality traits than when they shared positive ones.

8 Gently stroke them.

When you touch someone so gently that they hardly perceive it, it is subliminal touching. For instance, stroking someone's arm or patting their back might make them feel more kindly toward you.

Young guys chatted with ladies who were walking by while standing on street corners in a French research. When the males conversed with the women while softly touching their arms as opposed to doing nothing at all, they were twice as likely to succeed in starting a discussion.

In an experiment conducted by the University of Mississippi and Rhodes College, some servers briefly touched clients' hands or shoulders while they were handing back their change in order to study the impact of interpersonal contact on restaurant tipping. It turned out that the waitresses got far bigger tips than the ones who didn't interact with the clients.

9. Smile

In University of Wyoming research, over 100 undergraduate women saw photographs of another woman in one of four poses: smiling with the mouth open, smiling with the mouth closed,

not smiling with the mouth open, or not smiling with the mouth closed. No matter where she was positioned in the picture, the lady seemed to be most appreciated when she was grinning.
More recently, researchers at Stanford University and the University of Duisburg-Essen discovered that when an avatar smiled more, students who engaged with each other through avatars felt better about the encounter.

10. Consider how the other person wants to be seen.

People desire to be seen in a manner that supports the ideas they have about who they are. The self-verification hypothesis may be used to explain this phenomenon. Whether our beliefs are good or bad, we all want confirmation.
For a series of studies at Stanford University and the University of Arizona, participants with positive and negative opinions of themselves were asked if they wanted to interact with people who had positive or negative opinions of them.
Individuals who had favorable self-views preferred compliments from others, whereas participants who had

poor self-views chose criticism. This could be the case because individuals prefer to communicate with those whose input is compatible with their established identities.

According to another study, we get along better with individuals when their opinions of us mirror our own. We feel understood, which is a crucial element of closeness; therefore, that's probably why.

12. Let them in on a secret.

One of the strongest relationship-building strategies is self-disclosure.

College students were divided into pairs and instructed to spend 45 minutes getting to know one another as part of a study conducted by academics at the State University of New York at Stony Brook, the California Graduate School of Family Psychology, the University of California, Santa Cruz, and Arizona State University.

Some student pairings were given a set of more probing and intimate questions by the experimenters. For instance, "How do you feel about your connection with your mother?" was one of the intermediate questions. Other pairings were given questions meant for small conversation. For instance, one question was, "Which holiday is your favorite?" Why?"

The students who had asked progressively intimate questions during the trial felt significantly more connected to one another than the students who had just made casual conversation.

As you grow to know someone, you may use this method independently. For instance, you may go from simple inquiries (such as what movie they just watched) to finding out about the people in their lives that matter the most to them. Someone is more likely to feel closer to you and want to confide in you in the future if you share sensitive information with them.

12. Show that you can keep their secrets safe as well.

According to two studies conducted by scientists at the University of Florida, Arizona State University, and Singapore Management University, individuals place a high value on relationships that are both trustworthy and trustworthy.

These two characteristics turned out to be very significant when participants were visualizing their ideal buddy and coworker.

"Trustworthiness comprises several components, including honesty, dependability, and loyalty, and while each is important to successful relationships, honesty and dependability have been identified as the most vital in the context of friendships," writes Suzanne Degges-White of Northern Illinois University on PsychologyToday.com.

13. Show your sense of humor.

Regardless of whether participants were considering their ideal buddy or romantic partner, research from Illinois State University and California State University at Los Angeles indicated that having a sense of humor was crucial.

In a separate study, researchers from DePaul University and Illinois State University discovered that using humor while getting to know someone may increase their liking of you.In fact, the research found that taking part in a comical activity—for instance, having someone wear a blindfold while the other teaches them a dance—can boost romantic attraction.

14. Allow them to introduce themselves.

Recently, Harvard researchers found that, similar to food, money, and sex, talking about oneself may be intrinsically satisfying.

In one study, participants were asked to answer questions regarding either their own or another person's views while seated in an fMRI scanner. A friend or family member waiting outside the fMRI machine had been requested to attend the study with the participant. Participants were sometimes informed that their answers would be shared with a friend or family member, while other times they would be kept secret.

The findings demonstrated that individuals' motivation and reward-related brain areas were most active when they shared information with others, but they were equally engaged when they spoke about themselves in private.

In other words, if you let someone talk about their life instead of droning on about yours, they might remember you more favorably.

15. Show some vulnerability.

In an article on PsychologyToday.com, Jim Taylor of the University of San Francisco contends that emotional openness—or a lack thereof—can explain whether two individuals connect or not.

But Taylor acknowledges:

Making oneself vulnerable and not knowing whether this emotional exposure would be welcomed and reciprocated or rejected and diverted are dangers associated with emotional openness, of course.

The same Illinois State University and California State University in Los Angeles research mentioned above revealed that expressiveness and openness are crucial and desirable qualities in ideal mates, so it could be worth the risk. It doesn't matter whether that companion is a friend or a romantic one.

16. Pretend to like them.

Reciprocity of love is a psychological phenomenon that describes the tendency to like someone when we believe they like us.

For instance, participants were informed in a 1959 study published in Human Relations that certain participants in a group discussion would probably appreciate them. The researcher randomly assigned these individuals to these groups.

Those who claimed to like them were the people who the debate participants said they liked the best.

More recently, scientists from the Universities of Waterloo and Manitoba discovered that when we anticipate someone accepting us, we behave friendlier toward them, boosting the likelihood that they would in fact like us. Therefore, even if you're unsure of how someone else feels about you, behave as if you do, and chances are good that they'll feel the same way.

Chapter 4

One way to win people over to your way of thinking is to avoid arguing.

Avoid conflicts the same way you would avoid earthquakes or rattlesnakes. Most of the time, they'll merely harm someone's pride and make them feel inferior to you by making them feel uncomfortable, ashamed, or wounded.

Dale Carnegie had an acquaintance who sold trucks. Due to his many arguments with clients who had complaints or criticisms of the trucks he was selling, he didn't sell many vehicles. The salesperson improved to become one of the greatest salespeople his firm had ever seen after Dale urged him to put an end to the argument. If a person said, "I don't want a white truck! I'm heading to (an unknown firm) to purchase a vehicle! The truck salesperson may agree with the other salesperson that the competitor's vehicle was indeed an excellent truck and may praise its features.Then he would return and discuss the white truck's excellence, which was what he was attempting to promote.

Arguments never resolve misunderstandings; instead, tact, diplomacy, reconciliation, and a compassionate effort to understand the other person's perspective do.

When someone attempts to argue with you and makes a point you hadn't considered, acknowledge it and continue the conversation.

When you sense an argument is about to break out, resist the urge to act on impulse. When we feel we need to protect ourselves or a certain position, we may respond angrily. It may sometimes bring out the worst in us.

Manage your emotions. First, listen. Give them an opportunity to speak so that you may attempt to comprehend. Search for points of agreement. Express regret for any mistakes you may have made throughout the argument. Set pride aside.

Make a sincere commitment to thoroughly consider and research the arguments of your rivals. In order to avoid saying "I tried to tell you, but you wouldn't listen," it is best to

investigate and discover what your opponent may be saying.
Thank your opponents for listening to what you had to say and for striving to make improvements. Consider delaying a discussion or disagreement for a day so that both of you can calm down and collect information. gives you both more time to consider each other's arguments and decide whether or not the disagreement is worthy of your friend's pride. What would you stand to lose if you won the debate? Avoiding arguments is the only way to receive the greatest results from them.

How to Easily Create Enemies and Prevent Them

A person's intellect, dignity, and self-respect are all directly insulted when they are told they are incorrect. They don't want to agree with you as a result; they want to fight back.
Try not to tell anybody what you are going to prove if you can help it. Make sure no one knows you're doing it by being subtle and skillful with it.
"Men must be taught as if you had never taught them, and unknowns must

be offered as if they had been forgotten," said Alexander Pope.
Saying something like, "Well, now, see, I thought differently, but I may be wrong," when someone makes a claim that you KNOW is false is a good strategy. I am quite frequently.and I want to be corrected if I'm mistaken. Let's review the information. Using the phrase "I might be mistaken." A phrase like "Let's analyze the facts" may work miracles.

Respect others' ideas and be kind to them.

Admitting you could be mistaken can help you stay out of trouble. That will put an end to all debates and motivate your opponent to treat everyone equally and be just as accepting of the possibility that he may also be mistaken.
Never correct someone who is mistaken about anything. Put your diplomatic skills to work for you. Respect the other person's viewpoints. Do not ever say, "You're mistaken."

Admit When You're Wrong.

Be modest and say things about yourself that you know the other person wants to say or plans to say. If you do this, people may see you more favorably and downplay your errors in judgment.

Accepting responsibility for mistakes may be satisfying to a certain extent. It eliminates the sense of defensiveness and guilt while also assisting in the resolution of the issue brought on by the mistake. If you are mistaken, say so right away and forcefully.

Honey Drops

When you become angry and tell someone a few things, you may feel fine afterwards, but how does the other person feel? After you made them feel bad and insulted their dignity, do they want to accept your arguments?

"Let's sit down and take counsel together, and if we differ from each other, understand why it is that we differ, just what the points at issue are, and we will soon find that we are not so far apart after all, that the points on which we differ are few and the points on which we agree are many, and that if we only have the patience to wait, we will find that we are not so far apart after all." Wilson, Woodrow

Therefore, if you want to persuade a guy to support your cause, you must first show him that you are a true friend.

Engineer O.L. Straub needed to reduce his rent, or he wouldn't be able to pay it. He spoke to the landlord about how much he appreciated the apartments and what a fantastic job O.L. had done operating the property, rather than entering and attempting to debate pricing or how absurdly expensive the rent was. Then he said that he intended to remain for an additional year but was unable to do so financially. Even though he was famously tough to work with, the landlord went above and beyond to assist O.L. in securing a lower and more reasonable rent. Begin by being cordial.

Socrates' Secret

Never start a conversation with someone by bringing up a point on which you two disagree. Instead, focus on the things you have in common and keep mentioning them. If at all possible, keep stressing that you are both working toward the same goal and that the only thing separating you is procedure, not purpose. Keep having your opponent respond with "yes, yes" rather than "no." Once in the "no" condition, one will make an effort to stick to it in order to maintain their pride.

A persuasive speaker will first get a lot of "yes" replies. This gets the listeners' psychological responses going in the right direction.

It takes a lot of work and discernment to attempt to turn a prickly negative into a positive once one is in the "no" stage.

Ask questions that your opponent must answer in the affirmative (yes!). Continue to get acceptances one after another until you have a large number of affirmations on which to build, maybe leading your opponent to believe that your side is correct rather than theirs. Get the other person to instantly respond, "Yes, yes."

The Safety Valve in Handling Complaints

Most individuals who are attempting to convince others of their point of view speak too much themselves. Let the other individual resolve his or her own issues. They are far more knowledgeable than you about their company and its issues. Ask them questions and listen to their answers.

Keep quiet if you disagree with them. Let them complete it. If you interrupt them, they will continue to think in a flood of thoughts.

Encourage them to communicate completely. In interviews or while establishing rapport, keep in mind that almost every successful person enjoys talking about his early hardships. "If you want to develop enemies, outperform your friends." If you want friends, let your friends outperform you.To put it another way, support your pals. Pay attention to their successes. Don't extol your own virtue. Only mention your accomplishments when prompted. Leave most of the talking to the other person.

How to Procure Coordination

Most individuals want to feel as if they are making their own decisions and not being told what to do or sold anything. Make the individual feel as if the idea is theirs. Request their opinions or guidance on a subject. Make the other person feel as if the idea is theirs.

A Method That Will Be Effective for You

Remember not to judge someone for being incorrect, even if they are completely wrong. The prudent attempt was to comprehend this person's motivations for saying such a thing.

Put yourself in their position and attempt to understand why they behave in a certain way or why they would say what they said.

Consider the viewpoint of that individual and why they would wish to adopt yours. Consider how they might like to hear what you have to say. Try to honestly consider other people's perspectives.

What Everyone Wants

"I don't blame you one iota for feeling the way you do," is a saying that removes hostility, fosters good will, and improves people's listening to you. Without a doubt, if I were you, I would feel the same way. If you genuinely WERE that person, with their thoughts, sentiments, and history, you would truly FEEL that way; therefore, you can also say this with complete honesty. Obviously, your perspective would change if you were in their body.

Keep in mind that most people don't get much credit for being who they are. That is determined by things like their environment and upbringing.

The majority of individuals you encounter want to be understood. If you give it to them, they'll adore you.

Before responding to someone who has upset you or is arguing with you, try to react differently than anyone else would.Instead of reacting like an idiot, behave as a smart person would. Be understanding of the thoughts and aspirations of others.

Appealing Things That Everyone Appreciates

According to J. Pierpont Morgan, everyone has two reasons for doing something: one that sounds wonderful and the other that is their true motivation.

Although the individual may already be aware of the true cause, you don't need to stress it. Instead, make a more noble argument (one that will win over your opponent, client, employer, etc.). Give them strong reasons to accept the proposition about which you are attempting to persuade them.

For instance, John D. Rockefeller used higher ideals to persuade newspaper photographers to cease photographing his children. He simply remarked, "You know how it is, lads," rather than "I don't want these images taken." Some of you have children of your own. And you are aware that too much publicity is bad for children. arouse higher motivations

The Cinema Do it. TV does it. Why don't you try it out?

Dramatization: The truth must be compelling, captivating, and dramatic... You must use showmanship. If you want attention, do this.

This does not include lying, but rather speaking in a way that emphasizes the significance of what you are saying or attempting to get across. Dramatize what you say.

If Everything Else Fails, Try This

Encourage rivalry for the sake of striving for excellence rather than for financial gain. People like the opportunity to convey who they are, how important they are, and what they are worth. Several phrases to use to encourage completion include:

I had no idea you were slothful, a coward, a quitter, etc.

"You are correct. I doubt you ought to enroll in the course. Only intelligent individuals can pass the course.

Chapter 5

Change people without offending them or making them angry.

If you have to point out anything wrong, start here. Start out with sincere kudos and thanks. It is usually easier to listen to negative things after we have been complimented on our positive qualities.Commencing with praise is similar to a dentist starting his job by administering Novocain. Although the patient is still given a drill, Novocain provides pain relief.

How to criticize without drawing ire

Indirectly draw attention to other people's errors. Many critics start off with heartfelt compliments, followed by the word "but," and then they close with a critical comment. For instance, we may tell a youngster, "We're incredibly pleased with you for boosting your grades this term," in an effort to improve their carefree attitude about study. But the outcomes would have been better if you had put more effort into your mathematics. Until he heard the word "but," the youngster in this situation could have been inspired. The initial praise's genuineness could subsequently come under his scrutiny. The word "but" might be simply replaced with "and" to solve this. We're very happy with you for improving your grades this semester, and if you put in the same diligent work next semester, your math grade will be on par with everyone else's. Since there was no more indication of failure, the youngster would now accept the praise.

First, discuss your own errors.

Before you criticize someone else, discuss your own errors. Even if one hasn't fixed them, admitting one's own errors might persuade someone to alter his conduct. Nobody enjoys following directions.

Instead of providing directions directly, make inquiries.

Even if a reckless command was made to remedy a clearly undesirable situation, the resentment produced by it may last for a long time.

Whose vehicle is obstructing the driveway? a teacher barged into the room, asking indignantly. The teacher said, "Move the vehicle and move it right now, or I'll put a chain around it and haul it out of there," when the student who owned the car answered. Now we know that the pupil was mistaken. It wasn't appropriate to leave the automobile there. But from that point on, not only did that student dislike the instructor's behavior, but every student in the class did all they could to make the teacher's work difficult. What other way would he have handled it? The student would have happily moved the vehicle, and neither he nor his classmates would have been unhappy and resentful if he had inquired in a kind manner, "Whose car is in the driveway?" and then offered that if it were moved, other cars could go in and out.

In addition to making an order more appetizing, asking questions often inspires the ingenuity of the people you ask. If a person participated in the decision that led to the order's issuance, they are more inclined to accept it.

Allow the other person to keep his or her face.

Allowing one to keep their face!How incredibly necessary and significant that is! And how few of us ever give it any thought? When we insist on having our way, find fault, make threats, or criticize a kid or an employee in public, we often disregard the pain it does to the other person's pride. Though a few minutes, a few kind words, and a sincere appreciation of the other person's perspective would go a long way toward easing the pain! Even if we are completely correct and the other person is clearly mistaken, we only hurt someone's ego by making them look bad.Antoine de Saint-Exupery, a renowned French novelist and aviation pioneer, declared: "I have no right to say or do anything that lowers a man in his own eyes." What he believes about himself is more important than what I think of him. A man's dignity must not be violated.

How to motivate individuals to succeed

Praise any progress, no matter how little it may be. "Be liberal in your praise and hearty in your acclaim," the Bible says.

The fundamental idea behind B.F. Skinner's teachings is the use of praise rather than condemnation. By doing tests on both humans and animals, this brilliant psychologist has shown that when criticism is downplayed and praise is prioritized, positive traits in individuals are reinforced while negative traits deteriorate due to a lack of attention.

Everyone enjoys receiving praise, but when it is specific, it appears genuine rather than something the other person says to make them feel good.Keep in mind that everyone craves praise and fame and will do everything to get it. However, no one desires dishonesty. No one wants flattery.

When talents are criticized, they wither; when they are praised, they flourish.

Put a decent name on a dog.

Give the other individual a good name to uphold. If you have that individual's respect and demonstrate that you appreciate them for some form of talent, you can easily lead the average person. In other words, if you want to develop someone in a given area, behave as though that quality already distinguished him or her from others.
"Give a dog a bad name, and you may as well hang him," goes an ancient proverb. However, if you give him a decent name, watch what happens!

Make the error look simple to fix.

Encourage people. Make it seem simple to fix the issue. When you tell your kid, spouse, or coworker that they are bad at something, don't have the talent for it, or are doing it incorrectly, you nearly completely eliminate all motivation to attempt to do better. The person will practice until the sun goes out of the window in order to succeed, but if you use the opposite strategy—be liberal with your encouragement, make the task seem simple to complete, and let the other person know that you have faith in his ability to do it—he will practice until the sun comes up.

Getting others to be happy to achieve what you desire

Make the other person happy to follow your suggestion. When it's time to alter attitudes or behaviors, a successful leader should keep the following tips in mind.

Be genuine. Never make a promise that you can't keep. Put the advantages to yourself out of your mind and focus on the advantages to the other person.

Clearly define what it is that you want the other person to do. Be understanding. Consider what the other person really wants. Take into account the advantages that individuals will experience if they follow your advice. Adapt those advantages to the other person's desires. Put your request in a way that will give the other person the impression that he will personally get something from it.